Tourists

by

Stephen Evans

"Travelling is a fool's paradise."

Ralph Waldo Emerson
Self-Reliance

For production permissions and other information, please contact Time Being Media LLC at:

info@TimeBeingMedia.com.

Cover photo courtesy of NASA.

Tourists: Stephen Evans – Fourth Edition

ISBN: 978-1-953725-66-0

Contents

A Visitor to Your Planet

A Play in One Act

"I never see a pretty gal in my life
But that she was a boatman's wife."

The Boatman's Dance
Traditional Song

Cast of Characters

Alien   An alien, who looks like a woman.

Man   A man, who looks like a man.

Scene

A seashore.

Time

Now.

.

Act I Scene 1

Setting: A seashore. There is a boat onstage, turned upside down, bow pointed downstage. It is weathered and a bit battered.

At Rise: The man is painting the boat.

The alien enters and watches him. He doesn't look at her.

ALIEN
I am a visitor to your planet.

MAN
Aren't we all?

She is dismayed by his non-reaction.

ALIEN
I come from another planet.

He still doesn't look at her.

MAN
Welcome.

ALIEN
You believe me?

MAN

I do.

ALIEN

I thought you might be shocked.

MAN

We get a lot of tourists here.

ALIEN

I have carefully chosen this form so as not to frighten you.

The man looks at her for the first time. For a really long time.

MAN

Good choice. Want to sit?

ALIEN

Thank you.

She sits.

ALIEN

What is your name?

MAN

Horatio. What is your name?

ALIEN

Barbie.

MAN

Let me guess. You have carefully chosen that name so as not to frighten me.

ALIEN

How did you know?

MAN
Just guessing. What's your real name?

ALIEN
I cannot pronounce it in this form. Shall I revert to my
true form?

He looks at her. Again, for a really long time.

MAN
Barbie will do. There's coffee in that thermos.

She takes the thermos, opens it, looks inside.

ALIEN
What is coffee?

MAN
A consumable liquid foodstuff to sustain energy.

She sniffs.

ALIEN
Ah. Starbucks. One just opened in my galactic sector.

She pours some in a cup and sips.

ALIEN
Nourishing. That is most generous.

MAN
You're welcome.

She sips again.

ALIEN
Aren't you having any?

MAN
Too much caffeine.

ALIEN
Then why do you bring it?

MAN
You don't think you're the first thirsty alien I've met
here, do you?

ALIEN
Ahh. Well, it's good.

MAN
Good.

ALIEN
That's what I said.

MAN
No, that was a monosyllabic response of genial
acknowledgement. It's a custom round here.

ALIEN
Ahhh.
    Pause
Good.

MAN
You'll get the hang of it.

    She stands.

MAN
So I suppose you want me to take you to my leader.

ALIEN
You watch a lot of 1950s science fiction movies, don't
you?

> MAN

Bugs Bunny cartoons.

> ALIEN

Ah yes. I have studied those. They made me a little afraid to contact you.

> MAN

Why?

> ALIEN

They were so violent. I wondered what kind of intelligent creatures could enjoy such tragic spectacles.

> MAN

They are supposed to be funny.

> ALIEN

What is funny?

> MAN

If I knew the answer to that, I wouldn't be working here.

> ALIEN

I don't understand.

> MAN

Funny is when you think something hurts but you know it really doesn't.

> ALIEN

How can you think something and know something else?

> MAN

That's another local custom.

The man continues painting.

ALIEN
Why are you doing that?

MAN
Needs doing.

ALIEN
How do you know?

MAN
It's my work.

ALIEN
What is work?

MAN
What needs doing.

ALIEN
I'm asking you.

MAN
I'm telling you.

ALIEN
What is my work?

MAN
Asking questions?

ALIEN
That is my work!

MAN
You're good at your job.

Long pause

MAN
Is this your first visit to this planet?

ALIEN
Yes. To any planet really. Any other planet. Of course
I have been on my planet. I wouldn't want you to
think I was planetless.

MAN
You have planetary written all over you. First visit,
eh?

ALIEN
Yes.

MAN
Well. We're happy to have you.

ALIEN
Thank you.

MAN
How long have you been here?

ALIEN
One solar revolution.

MAN
A year. That's quite a while for a first visit.

ALIEN
No. One revolution of your solar system around the
galaxy. About 230 million of your years.

MAN
I imagine the place has changed a bit.

ALIEN
Yes. For example the last time I stood in this spot it
was under the sea.

MAN
Wait a few years and it should look very familiar.

ALIEN
It will.

MAN
Why did you start with this planet?

ALIEN
Each biosphere has a unique rotational signature.
About 250 million years ago, the signal from this
planet changed drastically, as if your entire world
went from shouting to whispering. It was so abrupt—
taking less than a million or so years—we felt obligated
to investigate. Unfortunately it took about ten million
years for the signal to reach us, and then another ten
million for me to reach this planet.

MAN
You travel at the speed of light?

ALIEN
In my original form. In this form it would mess up my
hair. Plus my mass would increase substantially.

MAN
How does travel increase your mass?

ALIEN
Mass increases with velocity.

MAN
As slowly as I move, you'd think I'd just float away.

ALIEN
Actually you are moving quite rapidly. This planet
moves at 28 kilometers per second around your star.
This solar system moves at 200 kilometers per second
around this little galaxy. This galaxy moves at 112

kilometers per second towards the next galaxy. And so on.

MAN

I wouldn't worry. Your mass seems just fine.

ALIEN

Thank you.

MAN

Did you ever find out what happened? 250 million years ago?

ALIEN

Yes. Almost all of the life on this planet died.

MAN

I've heard of that. Our scientists call it the Great Extinction.

ALIEN

It is certainly larger than any of the extinctions I have witnessed.

MAN

How many have you seen?

ALIEN

I have been here for four major extinction events. Five if you count the current one.

MAN

The current one?

MAN

Yes, the current extinction event. You are now losing approximately 10,000 species per year. You should reach major extinction levels in just a few centuries. You should be proud of your achievement.

MAN

Why would we be proud? That's terrible.

ALIEN

Oh. I assumed you were doing it on purpose. Your species gives that impression.

MAN

I can see that.

ALIEN

You do seem to be making a noble sacrifice.

MAN

In what way?

ALIEN

Destroying yourselves to save your planet.

MAN

We're doing our best.

ALIEN

It did seem bad planning that you should take so many species with you. But then you are humans; we cannot expect too much.

MAN

I certainly don't. That's one reason I like being out here by myself.

ALIEN

I am disturbing you. Shall I leave?

MAN

No. Please don't. It's not often I get to talk to 230-million-year-old alien.

ALIEN

Oh I am not 230 million years old.

MAN
I thought you said...

ALIEN
No. I have no age really. Where I am from we have no time. So, no age.

MAN
No time like the present.

ALIEN
Precisely.

He goes on painting.

MAN
So. You've been here a while. What do you think?

ALIEN
About what?

MAN
Our planet. You must have formed some opinions.

ALIEN
I prefer not to think.

MAN
You definitely came to the right place.

ALIEN
I am here merely to observe carefully and bring information back to my civilization.

MAN
I see.

ALIEN
You are the actually first human I have spoken with.

MAN
Really?

ALIEN
It is real.

MAN
How did you manage to be here all this time and not speak to another human?

ALIEN
I was in New York City.

MAN
Ahh.

ALIEN
The shows were good. And the pizza.

MAN
I could be an alien.

ALIEN
You are a human.

MAN
Most of the time.

ALIEN
What are you the rest of the time?

MAN
An animal.

ALIEN
What's the difference?

Long pause. REALLY long.

> MAN

Credit cards.

> ALIEN

What is a credit card?

> MAN

A method of obtaining pizza.

> ALIEN

I have seen those. They were long and green.

> MAN

No, that's money.

> ALIEN

What is money?

> MAN

A method of obtaining credit cards.

> ALIEN

I see. A credit card is a method of obtaining pizza and money is a method of obtaining a credit card and pizza is a method of obtaining money.

> MAN

That's about right.

> ALIEN

It seems pointless.

> MAN

That's the point. The system is designed to keep us from observing carefully.

> ALIEN

I see.

MAN

Do you have credit cards and money where you're from?

ALIEN

No. But then we have no pizza, so we don't need them.

MAN

If you didn't have a credit card, how did you get pizza?

ALIEN

It was difficult at first. But I changed into this form and they seemed quite happy to give it to me.

MAN

For not having spoken to a human, you seem to know our language well.

ALIEN

Thank you. I speak 2,347,691 languages. But only 779, 261 fluently.

MAN

That is a lot.

ALIEN

I have time too. Now.

MAN

I didn't know there were that many languages.

ALIEN

All substances have language. Quartz is my favorite. It is simple and pure. Willow is very complex.

MAN

And sad?

ALIEN
Yes. Do you speak willow?

MAN
I speak sad.

ALIEN
Most languages are simpler than yours. Your language
causes me great difficulty.

MAN
Why?

ALIEN
It changes so much.

MAN
Your language doesn't change?

ALIEN
Never. But then we don't have words.

MAN
How can you have a language without words?

ALIEN
Once we had words. But they just seem to confuse
everyone.

MAN
So do you communicate telepathically? Mind to mind.

ALIEN
No. We have one word that means everything and
never ends. And we each speak our part of it.

MAN
Conversation must be difficult.

ALIEN

It is impossible.

MAN

I think I might like your world.

Pause.

MAN

So how did you happen to pick me to speak to?

ALIEN

You were alone.

MAN

Can't argue with that.

ALIEN

You seemed to have some time.

MAN

Can't argue with that either. Time I have.

ALIEN

Do you wish to?

MAN

Have time? No one has ever asked me that. I suppose
I do. Not much that I would rather have than time,
come to think of it.

ALIEN

No. I mean. Do you wish to argue?

MAN

Oh. Hmm. Not really.

ALIEN

I would argue with you if you wish. I have never
argued with a human before.

MAN

That's thoughtful of you. But no.

ALIEN

There was something in your voice, as if you missed arguing.

He pauses.

MAN

I don't miss arguing. I suppose. I suppose sometimes I miss the person I used to argue with.

ALIEN

I see. Then arguing is a beneficial ritual between humans.

MAN

It can be. In the right circumstances it leads to making up.

ALIEN

Ah. We could argue and then make up. If you like.

MAN

I don't think we know each other well enough. But as we say, time will tell.

ALIEN

Who is we? Is this your social concatenation?

MAN

I never did know who we was. And I'm not sure I think too much of we anyway.

ALIEN

Then let us not speak of we if we do not please you.

The man gets up, stands back, and observes his

work. The alien stands back with him and does the same. He nods. She nods too. The man goes back and paints for a while.

ALIEN
What is this work?

MAN
I'm painting my boat.

ALIEN
Why do you do that?

MAN
Needs doing.

ALIEN
I would be pleased to not have that discussion again.

MAN
You are very polite for an alien.

ALIEN
Are not most aliens polite?

MAN
They are not impolite. But most of the time they don't talk to me. They just sit and watch the sunrise or sunset.

ALIEN
Yes. You are very lucky on this planet. Most planets do not have such colorful displays. Either the atmosphere is too thin and there is simply a flood of light morning and evening. Or the atmosphere is too thick and the light cannot get through at all. Or the planet is too close to the star and the light and heat

are too intense, or too far and they are barely
noticeable.

MAN
I guess we are lucky.

ALIEN
And this.

She points to the sea.
99.999 percent of the water in the universe is either
frozen or gas. There is more liquid water on this
planet than in all the rest of your galaxy combined.

MAN
I didn't know that.

ALIEN
This was a remarkable world.

MAN
Was? We still have the sea. We still have sunsets.

ALIEN
True. But soon you will not be around to enjoy them.

MAN
Point taken. What is your planet like?

ALIEN
There are no words in your language to describe it.

MAN
Ahh.

ALIEN
I could tell you in quartz.

MAN
When are you going home?

ALIEN

I don't know for sure. They were supposed to come pick me up 229 million years ago.

MAN

I'm sure they'll be here any minute.

She looks up.

ALIEN

It cannot be ruled out. But it is unlikely. We don't have minutes.

MAN

No minutes?

She shakes her head.

MAN

Days?

She shakes her head.

MAN

Solar revolutions?

ALIEN

No. As I said, we have no time. We have only now.

MAN

We have only have now here ourselves. We just like to pretend about days and minutes.

ALIEN

And solar revolutions.

MAN

Those too.

ALIEN

I guess it is 230 million years for me and now for them. Possibly this was a flaw in our planning.

MAN

Happens to the best of us.

Long pause.

MAN

Will you miss this planet when you go?

ALIEN

I will. I will miss the changingness. Is that a word?

MAN

It is now.

ALIEN

Will you?

MAN

Will I?

ALIEN

Will you miss this planet when you go?

MAN

A minute ago, I would have said yes.

ALIEN

Can so much change in a minute?

MAN

Not really. But now can change everything. As the willow would say.

ALIEN

True.

MAN

What if they never come for you? Will you die?

She points at him.

ALIEN

E.T. Great film.

MAN

Will you?

ALIEN

My people do not die. That is one reason I came. We do not understand why you would choose to die.

MAN

We don't choose to die. That's just life. You are born and you die.

ALIEN

This is the only planet in the universe where living beings die.

MAN

There is no death anywhere else?

ALIEN

No.

MAN

Huh. It never occurred to me there was any other option. I just thought that is what life was, everywhere. We come and we go.

ALIEN

I have watched countless creatures die in my time here. Whole species. Whole collections of species. I have observed most carefully each time, trying to understand the reason. But after 230 million years, I still do not understand.

MAN

Do you have religion on your planet?

ALIEN

Religion. You mean pre-determined rituals for communing with imaginary beings?

MAN

No. That would be marriage. I mean worship of a divine order.

ALIEN

There is no order in the universe. I thought humans knew that.

MAN

Why would you think that?

ALIEN

You act that way.

MAN

Fair point.

ALIEN

There cannot be order where there is no multiplicity. All only is, or can ever be.

MAN

Amen.

ALIEN

On my planet we worship no order, divine or otherwise.

MAN

Then how do you maintain a society?

ALIEN

We're just nice.

MAN

I see. So you don't have time and you don't have death and you don't have religion.

ALIEN

No.

MAN

Then you don't have an afterlife?

ALIEN

Afterlife?

MAN

A transition to a better place after death.

ALIEN

No we have no such thing. Do you?

MAN

It's one of those things we think but know something else. No death anywhere else. I wonder why we have death?

ALIEN

I do have one possible guess. But you must not tell anyone. I am not supposed to draw conclusions.

MAN

Don't worry. I'll be dead soon.

ALIEN

True.

MAN

So what is your guess?

ALIEN

It is the changingness. No other world has death, and no other world has the changingness. One is the price of the other.

MAN

Death is the price of change?

ALIEN

No. Change is the price of death. There is so much death here. It must be a good thing. Perhaps it is this afterlife. Perhaps the afterlife is something you know but do not think.

MAN

I suppose I'll find out soon enough.

ALIEN

Not if you come with me.

MAN

Come with you?

ALIEN

You could come with me.

MAN

I could?

ALIEN

I offer you a part of my word. That is a beneficial ritual where I come from.

MAN

I would live forever?

ALIEN

You would live now.

MAN
So if you can't die, what do you do?

ALIEN
Mostly we remember.

MAN
Remember. What will you remember about this planet?

Long pause.

ALIEN
Pizza.

MAN
I can see that.

ALIEN
And sunsets. And seashores. And you.

MAN
I would like to be remembered. You know, I think I would like to be remembered more than I would like to remember.

ALIEN
We all have our work.

He paints the last brushstroke.

MAN
Done.

ALIEN
You are finished?

MAN
Almost. I just need a name.

ALIEN
You have a name.

MAN
No. I need a name for my boat.

ALIEN
I don't suppose boats frighten you.

MAN
No.

ALIEN
So you would not need to carefully choose the name
so as not to frighten yourself.

MAN
No.

ALIEN
Then how do you choose a name?

MAN
That is a good question. The name of a boat is very
important. Your boat keeps you alive. It keeps you
fed. It keeps you free. A boat is a unique and special
creature. And the name has to reflect that.

ALIEN
You have chosen a name, haven't you?

MAN
I have.

He paints the name Barbie.

ALIEN
That is my name.

MAN

It is.

ALIEN

You won't get confused?

MAN

I may. But I'm used to it. It is my natural state as a human.

ALIEN

You painted it upside down. Perhaps that will help you tell us apart.

MAN

I painted it right-side up. It is the boat that is upside down.

ALIEN

I am relieved. It seemed a flaw in your planning. But I didn't wish to mention it.

MAN

Thank you.

The man stands back again and observes his work. The alien stands back with him and does the same. He nods. She nods too.

MAN

Okay then.

ALIEN

So now you have finished your work.

MAN

Yes.

> ALIEN

Then let us go.

> MAN

Where?

> ALIEN

Where do you think?

They look up. Then look at each other.

> TOGETHER

Pizza!

They start to leave.

> ALIEN

Do you have a credit card?

Blackout

The End

STEPHEN EVANS

At the Still Point

A Play in Two Acts

*"The only way of catching a train that I have discovered
is to miss the train before."*

–G. K. Chesterton

Cast of Characters

GWEN   A Grace Kelly look-alike (more the actress than the princess despite her 60 years)

ART   Gwen's age, a writer, more William Powell than Robert Redford.

MERLE   The station vendor, who looks a little bit like the Princeton version of Einstein (sweatshirt and sneakers included).

NARRATOR   A voice. The actors act out the narrated action as the voice speaks.

Setting: A train station.

Time: Late.

Act I

MERLE

Hey Lady.

NARRATOR

Gwen twists around on the wooden bench with no difficulty, since it had been worn smooth, almost polished, likely over many years as a resident of the tiny railway station that had been built mid-previous century, a small open space with a vaulted roof, two ticket windows (now closed), and a single vendor's cart near the door that offers newspapers, coffee, packaged treats, and souvenirs with the single vendor standing behind it, also likely a resident since mid-previous century. She thinks it odd that she has to do so, though, because for some reason, all of the benches in the station face away from the door that leads to the tracks, as though whoever designed the station had wanted arrivals and departures to come as a surprise. It makes no sense, but also she suspects it makes no sense to change it, as the tiny station in the small town where she grew up likely had little traffic anyway, and the benches seldom any occupants. Trains it seems to her are a remnant of past lives and past civilizations. Perhaps that is why she likes them.

The voice (both grating and filled with joy like a dark chocolate cupcake with orange cream inside) that summons her attention is both unexpected and mysteriously appropriate to the face that gazes at her over a newspaper crossword puzzle, pencil in hand, which reminds her a little bit of the Princeton version of Albert Einstein (sweatshirt and sneakers included). The accent is eastern European by way of the Bronx, with some other mysterious almost Celtic possibly Welsh influence wending its way through the vowels. Gwen, a Grace Kelly look-alike, though more the actress than the princess despite her 60-some years, had travelled extensively, as perhaps most Grace Kelly look-alikes have the opportunity to do, tries to imagine the life journey that could concoct such a voice and is actually startled when the voice burbles again.

MERLE
What's an eight-letter word for unusual? Starts with a U. Not unusual. Well, unusual does. But unusual but not unusual. If you get me.

GWEN
Unwonted.

MERLE
No, this one has an o in it.

GWEN
Unwonted.

MERLE
Ah. Unwanted. Got ya.

NARRATOR
Albert nods. Though his name probably is not Albert, since Albert would not be asking her questions, both because he was Albert and more importantly because he had died before she was born.

MERLE
How do you spell that?

GWEN

U-N-W-O-N-T-E-D. As in unwonted silence.

MERLE

Ah. Unwonted. Got ya. Thanks.

(Pause)

MERLE

Hey Lady.

NARRATOR

Gwen puts down the book and swivels again, smiling.
Gwen always smiles at strangers, especially when she
is alone with them in a deserted train station. But she
feels no alarm. Immediately on entering the station
she had determined, with a sureness that in a life of
many encounters had almost never failed her, that
Albert was no threat to her, nor likely to anyone
except the yellow wooden pencil he was gnawing
between bouts of interrupting her attempted reading.

MERLE

When's your train?

NARRATOR

Gwen glances up at the large clock on the wall, which
says 11:55, as it has for the last two hours. The chimes
at midnight will never be heard, she thinks. Cinderella
need never fear for her pumpkin and four.

GWEN

Soon.

(To herself)

I hope.

MERLE
Want some coffee? On the house. Not much busy
tonight.

GWEN
I don't drink coffee this time of night. But thanks.

MERLE
Snickers? Chips. I got chips. Gum. Cigarettes. Except
you can't smoke in here. Used to. Used to you could
smoke. Some days you could hardly breathe. I been
here thirty-four years, right in this booth. Well, I
mean I go home. But I've been working here thirty-
four years. I inherited from my uncle. He was here
twenty-seven years, right when they opened this
place. Used to be busy here. Once upon a time those
benches were filled, with commuters mostly. Coming
and going. Coming and going. Somedays I'd sell so
much gum or candy or mints or newspapers or
cigarettes, I didn't even have time to finish my
crossword. These days, not so many trains, or people,
or money. Still I get by. And I finish my crossword.
Thirty-four years. I've seen some things. Learned
some things. Though I still haven't figured out why
the benches face away from the train tracks. It's like
they want people to strain their necks. I shouldn't
complain. I sold a lot of aspirin too. Ordinarily I
would be closed up and going home by now. But I
never abandon a customer. It's my code.

GWEN
I imagine things have changed in thirty-four years.

MERLE
You'd think so, wouldn't you? But not so much. That
clock on the wall? That clock has said 11:55 since

2011. But people still look at it. I guess they have
hope. In thirty-four years, that is one thing I have
learned. There is always hope in a train station. Hey
lady?

GWEN
Mints. I'd like some mints.

MERLE
Stay there. I'll bring.

NARRATOR
Albert carefully considers before selecting a pack of
wintergreen mints. He strolls up one aisle and across
another before reaching her side. Gwen opens the
package, shakes a mint into her hand, and pops it into
her mouth.

MERLE
I'm Merle.

GWEN
Gwen.

NARRATOR
Merle who is not Albert slides down onto the bench,
though at a respectful distance, and stares at the wall
in front of them. The building itself is round, with
twelve tall windows set at even intervals around the
circumference. During the day, the arched windows
above their heads might have allowed some light
despite the decades of grime that had accumulated.
But at this hour, neither moonlight nor starlight nor
streetlight penetrate the murky glass. The high ceiling
lamps of ancient incandescent design, reflecting dimly
as if they were embedded in windows turned night
mirrors, seem almost like a time tunnel, offering a

view into a vanished era of Myrna Loys and Clark Gables.

> GWEN

Mint?

> MERLE

I better get back to my crossword. I like to finish it by the time I leave.

> GWEN

Good for you. I never finished one in my life.

> MERLE

If you don't stop, eventually you finish. You have a good trip.

> GWEN

Thank you.

> NARRATOR

Merle unwinds more than stands, his lower body only reluctantly following the upper, then shuffles back toward his cart. Gwen quickly spits the mint into her hand and squints to see if there is a Use By date on the package. She turns again to see if Merle has noticed, and sees instead William Powell (minus the mustache) standing in the doorway watching her.

William (whose name is Art) is tall, well over six feet, and had been she remembers since high school, though his shoulders then stooped a bit to try to hide it, and himself. The attempt had not been successful back then; no one missed him when he walked into a room. But he must have gotten better at it over the years, or something had settled into him that rendered him not less present, he was still present, but less knowable, as if the appearance was just that:

simulation. Façade. Well, we all have that by now, she thinks. But in Art it has become something more, almost a personality to be worn more than a disguise to be adopted.

As these thoughts race through her mind, she sees he has been making the same evaluation of her, and wonders what he has concluded. But he doesn't turn and leave. That is something, and she would not have blamed him after all this time. He must be curious. He always had been, about everything, and she had labored to pull him away from his books into her world.

He glides toward her, navigating the aisles and spaces between the benches with a practiced grace, as if he ran mazes for a living.

She leans down and surreptitiously slides his book into her bag before he rounds the last turn of the maze. When he reaches her, he stands, smiling (at strangers in train stations she thinks and almost laughs). Neither of them is in a hurry. They enjoy the beginnings of whatever this is for a moment longer, lost in the spell of what had been, and what might have been, before what never was intervened.

GWEN
I didn't know if.

ART
It's not often I get an invitation from the past.

NARRATOR
She looks down, as if shy, though that was something she had never been and isn't now and yet she looks

down all the same and wonders briefly why he brings this out in her.

GWEN

Really? I get them all the time.

NARRATOR

He gestures to the bench. She rearranges her bag and scoots a bit. He sits. He isn't smiling now. He isn't even there. She wonders where he is, in what age or era of their lives together, or perhaps just his own. She waits for him to come back. As she does, she restrains the urge to brush his hair back the way she used to, and wonders what urges have returned to him. Her wrist, she thinks. He liked to encircle her wrist with this thumb and forefinger. She hadn't thought of it for decades perhaps, and had never until now wondered why he did it, what it meant to him. Was she so delicate in his mind then he was afraid to break her? No, that was definitely not it. Was he trapping her, or feeling her pulse, ensuring she was real, or envisioning a ring he might one day offer? She didn't know, and didn't know if he would remember himself.

ART

I was surprised to get your call.

GWEN

I was surprised you had the same phone number.

ART

Some things don't change.

GWEN

Most things do. Until they change back.

ART
So. What brings you back here?

GWEN
The funeral.

ART
Not your Dad?

GWEN
No. He's still.

ART
I can imagine. I mean. Good for him. He must be...

GWEN
93 last January.

ART
So. Whose funeral?

GWEN
Izzy.

ART
Izzy. Who?

GWEN
She was in our class Senior year.

ART
Can't place her.

GWEN
She wasn't in our crowd.

ART
Ah. Did we have a crowd?

GWEN
More of gang. Gaggle. Pandemonium. Quiver.

ART

Quiver?

GWEN

Cobras.

ART

Ah. I want to ask how the funeral was. But it sort of answers itself.

GWEN

A lot of people there. I thought I might see you.

ART

Didn't hear about it.

GWEN

I think they should have funerals before you die. It seems rude to wait.

ART

It does, doesn't it?

GWEN

The nicest party you're ever invited to, and you really can't enjoy it.

ART

Weddings are nice. So I hear.

GWEN

You never?

ART

You?

GWEN

Twice. No. Three times. Depends on how you count.

ART

Does it?

GWEN
You and Izzy should have gotten together.

NARRATOR
Art shrugs, and it almost makes her laugh. Many
things almost make her laugh, but his shrug has
moved near the top of the list. She thinks of the train
moving down the track to take her away. No time for
another bad decision.

GWEN
I mean you live in the same small town. You'd think
your paths would have crossed.

ART
I'm not much of a path-crosser. How about you?

GWEN
No. Except at funerals. And train stations.

ART
Is that why we're meeting here? You know you have a
getaway scheduled?

GWEN
Maybe. And maybe I didn't want to spend my last
minutes in this town with Merle.

ART
Who?

GWEN
Mint?

ART
Uh. Sure.

GWEN
Hey Merle.

MERLE
Yes, Milady?

GWEN
You still have that coffee you mentioned? We could both use a cup.

MERLE
Sure.

ART
You always had a penchant for making friends.

GWEN
You always had a penchant for using words like penchant.

ART
So.

GWEN
So.

ART
Why am I here?

GWEN
Going existential already. I thought you grew out of that phase in Twelfth Grade.

ART
Turtlenecks and dark glasses never go out of style.

NARRATOR
Gwen reaches down into her bag. He looks over, curious to see what she is going for, then his eyes widen as she pulls out a book.

GWEN
I finished your last book.

ART
Ah. You were the one who bought it.

GWEN
It reminded me of you.

ART
Hopefully that's a compliment.

GWEN
A not uncomplicated one, but yes.

ART
That's fair to say.

GWEN
It seemed like one of the characters might have been based on me.

ART
Maybe. In a not uncomplicated way.

GWEN
We had a not uncomplicated time together.

ART
We're not uncomplicated people.

GWEN
Would you sign it for me?

ART
Sure. Do you have a pen?

GWEN
Oh.

ART
Don't worry. I have one.

GWEN

Then why did you ask?

ART

In Author school, we're taught not to seem too eager.
It's an image thing.

NARRATOR

He turns to the title page, writes something, signs it,
and hands it back. She examines the signature. It is
smoother now, more assured, yet somehow less
readable. She reads the inscription, then laughs.

GWEN

To not uncomplicated memories. Funny.

ART

They teach us that too. And how to look humble.

GWEN

Your handwriting has not improved.

ART

That they could not teach.

NARRATOR

Gwen takes one more glance at the inscription, then
puts the book away, burying it in her bag like treasure.

GWEN

I kept your letters.

ART

From when we were together or from when we
weren't?

GWEN

Both.

ART

I'm surprised they haven't turned to dust. Or been remaindered.

GWEN

Are you saying we're old and unwanted?

NARRATOR

Merle arrives behind them, bearing two light blue paper cups of coffee with dark plastic lids. He hands each of them a cup, then draws packets of sweetener and creamer out of seemingly every pocket and dumps them onto the space between them.

MERLE

U-N-W-O-N-T-E-D. As in unwonted silence. See I remember things.

GWEN

Crossword. Thank you, Merle.

MERLE

Sorry. It's been sitting a while.

GWEN

So have I.

MERLE

I can brew new!

GWEN AND ART

If only.

GWEN

This is fine. We just need something to cover the unwonted silences.

NARRATOR

Merle looks one to the other, and likes what he sees.
This is good, he thinks. Good things like this should
happen here. So much has happened here over thirty-
four years. Good things. Bad things. And mostly the
things that happen between them. But you should
notice the good things especially; that is his
philosophy. Privacy. Privacy and coffee are what are
needed.

MERLE

Actually I don't brew myself. I get from the coffee
shop next door. It's good. So I'll go borrow. You'll
watch my cart?

GWEN

Like two hawks.

ART

Are you expecting any?

GWEN

Coffee?

ART

Unwonted silences.

GWEN

No, just the wonted ones.

NARRATOR

They gaze at each other for a while, absorbing the
now, remembering the then, comparing the two.
When they are both too full of time, she takes a drink.
He does too. They grimace. Then both add lots more
cream and sugar.

ART

Well, I'm glad we got that out of the way.

GWEN

Me too.

ART

Walk?

GWEN

I still get around.

ART

Would you like to take a walk?

NARRATOR

She looks at his hand. No ink stains. All computerized now she imagines. It is a strong hand. It does not waver when extended towards her. But probably soft too. The fingers curve gently, beckoning. She has always noticed hands. Or maybe that is something she has learned. She does not remember his hands from years ago. Just the flat stomach and—other things.

GWEN

I would. But. My train should be here soon.

NARRATOR

She glances at the broken clock. The numbers, roman numerals, she corrects herself, barely visible through the round crystal face, have delicate green vines climbing up them, twining around them, like—she can't recall where she has seen that image before. Perhaps it was the style, she imagines, when the clock was new.

GWEN

That's the theory anyway.

NARRATOR
Art glances at the clock, then at her, then back at the
clock, then at his phone. Art takes a moment, saving
the detail to use in a story someday. The Stopped
Clock. The Broken Clock. Remembrance of Time
Stopped. The Day the Clock Stood Still. He returns to
reality.

GWEN
I think maybe it's the Doomsday clock. It hasn't
moved since I've been here, fortunately.

ART
Even a broken clock is right twice a day.

GWEN
Actually, a stopped clock is right twice a day. A
broken clock may never be right.

ART
Which do you think it is?

GWEN
We'll have to wait and see.

ART
True.

ART
Well, since we aren't facing imminent Armageddon,
how about a walk just around the station?

GWEN
Take a turn around the room? How Jane Austen of
you.

ART
I'm nervous.

                    GWEN
Why?

                    ART
I haven't been up this late in about 30 years.

                    GWEN
There is that. A turn it is. Shall we go armed?

                    NARRATOR
She picks up the coffee cups, and hands his to him,
then looks around her at the station.

                    GWEN
Clockwise or counterclockwise?

                    ART
With this clock, I'm not sure there is a difference.

                    GWEN
Good point. Left or right. Sunnyside or widdershins?
Upstream or downstream?

                    ART
Upstream. It's more literary.

                    GWEN
Born back ceaselessly into the past.

                    NARRATOR
Gwen laughs. In anyone else it might be called a
chuckle, but in her the action is too elegant. It is more
a delicate shift in the universe. Her hair tosses deftly,
and he notices, and she notices him noticing. She slips
her free arm in his and begins to stroll. He matches
her stride instinctively. But then he must be used to
shorter women, she thinks

ART
Are you going far?

GWEN
Just once around. As far as I know.

ART
Are you traveling far?

GWEN
Still asking existential questions.

ART
I meant your train. Not prying. Just wondering.

GWEN
You had a penchant for that too.

ART
Wondering where you live now.

GWEN
I'm between homes at the moment.

ART
You're homeless?

GWEN
No. I have five. I just don't know which to go to.

ART
Five homes? Why do you have five homes?

GWEN
Two and a half husbands times two.

ART
You know you can sell them. You don't have to keep them forever.

NARRATOR

Gwen pauses. They are at the point in a meeting of old friends where some account of the years is required, and she is not sure that at whatever time at night it is she has the energy. But she can see that he will not accept the short answer, and sighs.

GWEN

I hold onto them as a reminder of what I should never do again.

ART

That bad?

GWEN

Not in the living. Only in the remembering.

ART

I hate that.

GWEN

You too?

ART

Sort of.

NARRATOR

Art grimaces a bit, realizing himself that they have entered another and likely uncomfortable phase of revelation. The four horsemen soon to arrive, he thinks and nearly laughs, but then swings his head in something of a figure eight, evoking for himself the infinitude of his mild regrets.

ART

I'll write something.

GWEN

Seems like something a writer should do.

ART

You would think. In the moment, I'll be convinced
that it is the most brilliant thing I have ever written.

GWEN

And?

ART

And then I'll read it again later. In a year if I'm brave.
In five if I'm not.

GWEN

Not as good?

ART

Never.

GWEN

Not even once?

ART

Not even.

GWEN

How odd.

ART

Do you mind?

GWEN

I can't seem to help it.'

ART

I don't want to pry.

GWEN

It's my own fault. I invited you.

ART

I'm just curious. Never having...

GWEN
I understand. Ask.

ART
Divorced?

GWEN
One divorce, one widowing, one annulment.

ART
Annulment? They still do that?

GWEN
So my lawyer says.

ART
Why?

GWEN
He had another wife he forgot to mention.

ART
Ah. That's significant.

GWEN
Yes. It's not the good kind of threesome.

ART
I'm starting to feel a bit provincial here.

GWEN
Small town. And it's charming.

ART
Really?

GWEN
Don't tell me you don't know.

ART
I could never tell with you, how you felt about things.

NARRATOR
She lifts her hand, wanting to run it through his hair.
He has good hair. Ample. Seemingly undiminished.
She rescues him from some lint instead.

GWEN
As I recall, I made my feelings pretty clear.

ART
Well. That. Yes.

GWEN
A number of times.

ART
I remember.

GWEN
I sometimes wonder. If. Back then. If you had asked
me to marry you—

ART
I did.

GWEN
You might have saved me two and a half marriages
and five houses I don't like.

ART
I did ask.

GWEN
Or maybe it would be three and a half marriages and
seven houses. Who knows?

ART
I did ask you.

GWEN
Life takes these funny turns. Except I never seem to
laugh.

ART
Gwen. I did ask you to marry me.

NARRATOR
She stops underneath the recalcitrant clock, and
notices the clock face reflected in the darkened
windows throughout the station, though the wall on
which it hangs is not itself visible, so the clock
appears suspended in the air. Some trick, of the
hanging lights (which lights themselves are also
suspended in the dark like stars around the moon)
reflecting off the clock face or the wind outside
against the ancient windows or just her own tired
vision, makes it seem as if the hands of the mirrored
clock are turning now, but backwards. She tries to
work out whether a clock in a mirror would go
retrograde, working out the vectors of reflection. She
steps out a pace and glances up at the actual clock. He
joins her, looks up, sees the motionless clock, gives
her a questioning glance. She steps back against the
wall, tilts her head and squints a bit and the illusion in
the mirror resolves; the hands once more are still.
Then his words finally register.

GWEN
You did what?

ART
I did ask you to marry me.

GWEN
Are you sure?

ART

I'm positive.

GWEN

Were we stoned? It doesn't count if you're stoned.

ART

We were not stoned. It counted for me. The one and only.

GWEN

You're not joking?

ART

No.

GWEN

And it wasn't a joke then? That we maybe just laughed off.

ART

I did not laugh it off.

GWEN

Because we were only?

ART

I was 21. You were—

GWEN

(Quickly)
Younger. Hmmm. Really? Wow.

GWEN

Maybe I didn't like you as much as I remember.

ART

Apparently.

GWEN
Was I nice about it at least?

ART
You were. Sort of. You pretended it didn't happen.

GWEN
What?

ART
You went on talking about going to Europe for the summer.

GWEN
Really? I said nothing?

ART
Not about that. You talked about how you heard Prague was so beautiful and you couldn't wait to see the Volga.

GWEN
Vltava.

ART
Gesundheit.

GWEN
Funny. The Vltava flows through Prague.

ART
I didn't know that then.

GWEN
Probably neither did I.

ART
So we finished our dinner and I took you home.

GWEN
Did we break up?

ART
Not till you went to Europe that summer.

GWEN
A woman turns down your proposal of marriage and you still date her? What, have you no self-respect?

ART
The sex was really good.

GWEN
Oh. Well. Sure. You're a man. Wait. Where did this alleged proposal take place?

ART
Jake's Crab House.

GWEN
You're kidding. Did you want me to say no?

ART
Of course not. I thought it was romantic.

GWEN
You thought Jake's Crab House was romantic?

ART
We had been there several times. I thought of it as our place.

GWEN
You thought Jake's Crab House was our place?

ART
Apparently. At the time.

GWEN
Then I think we need a new place.

ART
Do we?

GWEN
I'm sure of it. Did you want me to say yes?

ART
Probably. I doubt that I thought through the alternatives.

GWEN
Oh. Well. Sure. You're a man. So you proposed to me at the noisiest restaurant on the East Coast. Did you get down on one knee?

ART
No. It was a crab house. The floor was a mess.

GWEN
Understandable. Was there a ring?

ART
There was. But I never got to that part.

GWEN
So I have a theory.

ART
Don't say it.

GWEN
You know what it is?

ART
I think so.

GWEN
I don't think I heard you.

ART
I don't think you did either.

GWEN
Wow.

ART
I know.

NARRATOR
Gwen looks into his eyes, so curious to see what she can see there. Mostly, there is humor. Then deeper, wonder at the question of the evening: what if? And behind that, understanding, that they have had their paths, and that those paths have brought them here. And somehow here in the station beneath the stopped or broken clock the question in both their minds is transformed, from what if?, to what now? And they both realize that, but neither knows how to face it, nor answer it.

GWEN
I mean.

ART
I know.

GWEN
Wow.

ART
I know.

GWEN
Can you imagine?

ART

Vividly. Every day. For several years.

GWEN

Poor boy.

ART

I had even spoken to your father beforehand.

GWEN

No!

ART

Yep. In my 20-year-old classic nerd mind, it was the right thing to do.

GWEN

What did my father say?

ART

He said good luck. In that way he had of saying, no way in hell but I respect you for asking.

GWEN

Yes. He could say a lot in a few words. Can say.

ART

He never told you about it?

GWEN

Never told, never asked. He liked you. He never said it. But he did. I could tell.

ART

Sure. He looked at me and thought: here is a boy who will never leave this town. And who could keep my Gwen here with him. And he was right, about the first part. I don't think anyone could have kept you here though.

>   GWEN
No.

>   ART
Did you ever think about moving back?

>   GWEN
No.

>   ART
Didn't think so.

>   GWEN
I mean. Our whole lives could have been different.
Our whole lives.

>   ART
Yes. Maybe. But who knows? Lives change every
minute. From the choices we make.

>   GWEN
Like restaurant selection.

>   ART
Like restaurant selection. And from the choices we
don't even think of as choices. Like asking me here.

>   GWEN
Like coming here?

>   ART
That too.

>   GWEN
I knew I was making a choice. After all these years, I
knew.

>   ART
So did I.

GWEN
What was the deciding factor?

ART
I suppose. Curiosity.

GWEN
Me too!

GWEN
It's mind boggling.

ART
It is.

GWEN
So.

ART
Yes?

GWEN
How long?

ART
Yes?

GWEN
How long have you held this theory that I never heard you?

ART
Since the next day.

GWEN
That's a long time.

ART
Almost—

GWEN

Oh let's not.

ART

Agreed.

NARRATOR

Gwen works her way through vague memories of the evening, remembering that the food was good but messy, the evening oddly short, no sex, not even a kiss as he dropped her home. She hadn't thought anything of it at the time; her mind filled with thoughts of Europe. Certainly at the time she had assumed he would accompany her, or join her at some point. She hadn't wanted to break up. She hadn't known they had until the day she left.

GWEN

Why didn't you say anything?

ART

What was I supposed to say? Oh by the way, did you hear my proposal of marriage?

GWEN

I see the problem.

ART

I did not want to go through it again.

GWEN

Even though you may not have gone through it the first time?

ART

I went through it. Apparently you didn't.

GWEN

I suppose.

ART

It was the most soul-crushing experience of my entire life. I was devastated. You know.

GWEN

Know what?

ART

At that age. How you feel things.

GWEN

That I remember. I'm so sorry.

ART

Thank you. Though.

GWEN

Yes?

ART

I am curious.

GWEN

So you said.

ART

I suppose that's why I came.

GWEN

Then ask.

ART

Now I'm not sure I want to know. I mean. Is it worth knowing, while knowing that it changes nothing?

GWEN

It changes nothing that has happened. But. You don't know that it would change nothing in the future. Or even. The now.

ART

Now that is existential. You must have learned it from me.

GWEN

Possibly.

ART

At the still point, there the dance is.

GWEN

Excuse me?

ART

T. S. Eliot.

GWEN

I thought so. For a moment, I thought you were asking me to dance.

ART

Only at the still point.

GWEN

It doesn't get more still than this.

ART

True. There's no music.

GWEN

The sound comes and goes. The music is always real.

ART

Who said that?

GWEN

You did. In one of your novels.

ART

Did I? Good line.

NARRATOR
He turns to her and offers her his hand. They
entwine, and dance, slowly. Perhaps there is music.
Perhaps there isn't. They don't seem to mind either
way.

Lights fade.

End Act 1.

STEPHEN EVANS

Act II

NARRATOR

Gwen and Art dance, in and out of the lights and shadow. They stop moving, but do not step back from each other.

GWEN

That was nice. I didn't mind no music.

ART

My heart was beating like a drum. Does that count?

GWEN

It was nice. Familiar. It reminded me.

ART

Yes?

GWEN

That you were a terrible dancer.

NARRATOR

The laughter creates some distance between them. But Art holds onto one of her hands.

ART

True. But when I danced with you, no one was looking at me.

GWEN

You're not going to propose again, are you?

ART

No. Are you disappointed?

GWEN

Possibly. I've had several, but I am curious how you would go about it.

ART
Not well, apparently. Considering.

GWEN
But maybe you learned something from the first
attempt.

ART
I don't think this is something where experience is a
help.

GWEN
True. It didn't help me, I can say that. So if you're not
proposing, what do you want to know?

ART
If you had heard? When I proposed?

GWEN
Yes?

ART
What do you think you would have said?

GWEN
Mint?

ART
Oh come on. I've waited mphmfh years for an answer.

GWEN
How could I possibly know now what I would have
felt then if?

ART
I know how I felt.

GWEN
How?

ART

I felt that no one else in the world could wear a
baseball cap as well as you. I felt that when you jogged
by my house in the morning with your ponytail
swinging side to side that the earth spun a little slower
just to give me more time to gaze at you in wonder. I
felt that when you shook your hair a certain way there
was air to breathe. I felt that when my arms were
around you I didn't need the air anymore and when
your hand was in mine my heart didn't need to beat. I
felt that when you passed by flowers leaned your way
and the grass turned greener just for you. I felt that
your silhouette just filled the empty space in my life
like one of those cartoon cutouts. I felt that when you
smiled a butterfly must be born somewhere because
that much beauty must have consequences.

GWEN

That's how you felt?

ART

Yes.

GWEN

Was that how you proposed?

ART

No. I think, when I proposed, I said something like: I
think we should get married. Don't you?

GWEN

That's what you said?

ART

There may have been an extra pause or two, but
pretty much.

NARRATOR

He can't look at her. He wonders if he will ever be able to look at her again, and then wonders if after tonight he will ever get another chance.

GWEN

But that other, the baseball cap and the running.

ART

Jogging.

GWEN

And the grass and the butterfly. You remember all that.

ART

I do.

GWEN

How?

ART

I wrote it down. First bit of writing I ever did.

NARRATOR

He takes out his wallet and unfolds a ragged piece of paper. She reaches for it. He doesn't let it go at first, but finally he does. She stares at the unfolded paper.

GWEN

And you kept it. All this time.

ART

Sort of.

GWEN

What do you mean—sort of?

NARRATOR

Art reaches for it. Gwen doesn't want to let it go, but she does. She then reaches to take it back again, but he doesn't give it to her.

ART

Well. I look at it. Once in a while.

GWEN

You look at it.

ART

Once in a while. After a few years, it wears out. So. I retype it. I still have my old typewriter and I found some of the same notepaper. So it looks the same.

GWEN

How many times have you retyped it?

ART

I don't know.

GWEN

Give me a ballpark number.

ART

Eight.

GWEN

Eight.

ART

Eight.

GWEN

So did you keep it because it reminded you of how you felt about me or because it was your first real piece of writing.

ART

The second one.

GWEN

Oh.

ART

I didn't need anything to remind me how I felt about you. And then I didn't want anything to remind me. And then it didn't remind me. Because I found I had it memorized.

GWEN

So I see.

ART

And then.

GWEN

Yes?

ART

And then it occurred to me that it was really good writing and I should use it. So I did. In a book.

GWEN

The one I just read.

ART

That's the one. That's what we authors do. We put things in books. And we try to disguise them, so no one knows who they are about.

GWEN

When I read it, I wondered if that was about me.

ART

Except sometimes the people they are about.

. GWEN

It made me curious. I think that's why I called. Maybe.
What took you so long?

ART

Excuse me?

GWEN

What took you so long? To put it in a book.

ART

It nearly went into every book I wrote. But I always
took it out. Until this one.

GWEN

Why this one?

ART

Because I could finally bear it. Gwen.

GWEN

Yes?

ART

Would you?

GWEN

Marry you? I heard that one.

ART

Would you like to have it?

GWEN

You don't want it anymore?

ART

I put it in a book. It's not mine now.

GWEN

Ah. Okay. Thanks. I would like to have it. Might be worth something someday, the first piece of writing by a famous novelist.

ART

You never know.

GWEN

I never did.

NARRATOR

There is a long pause. They both feel the energy has ebbed a bit, and that disappointment is seeping in in its place. Merle enters noisily. But they don't notice. He watches for a moment. Then bustles up, carafe in one hand, cups in the other. He hands each of them a round clear mug like a glass ball with the top open, then pours the liquid carefully.

MERLE

Looks like I'm just in time. Coffee, fresh. There. Now you're ready for another unwonted silence.

GWEN

You're really liking that word, aren't you?

MERLE

Why do you think I do crosswords? You're never too old. Well, that's not true. Sometimes you are. But you're never too old to think you're never too old.

GWEN

This is delicious. Thank you, Merle. Just what we needed.

ART

Yes, thank you. Our silences are now covered for the remainder of the evening. Morning. Whichever time this is.

MERLE

It's what I'm here for.

GWEN

Must be nice.

ART

What?

GWEN

To know what you're here for.

ART

You're here for a funeral.

GWEN

Am I?

ART

Aren't you?

GWEN

I suppose. A funeral. A commemoration. Of loss. And passage. Hey Merle, what's another word for funeral?

Merle
(Without looking up)
Exequy.

GWEN

How about a word for funeral song?

MERLE
(Without looking up)
Epicedium.

GWEN
Yes. That's why I'm here. An epicedium.

MERLE
(Still without looking up)
Your crossword is depressing.

GWEN
It is, isn't it?

ART
You're in a pensive mood.

GWEN
Is that the right word? Pensive?

ART
It must be. I'm a writer.

NARRATOR
Gwen nods again, which is what Art has been hoping
for. Her hair fluffs, just the bangs. He remembers the
bangs, how they fascinated him all those years ago,
and he still can't look away from them. Then she
shakes her head, which sends the hair in opposite
directions at once. Art begins composing a poem to
her bangs, which he will never write down because
it's too silly. Art nods back, wondering what his hair is
doing. He doesn't have bangs—his hair is brushed
straight back, revealing a massive forehead (evidence
he has always suspected of a massive brain behind it,
substantial evidence—including his presence here
tonight—to the contrary) that is probably slightly
damp and gleaming under the lofty lamps.

GWEN
Then I guess I am. No. I wouldn't say pensive.

ART
What would you call it?

GWEN
I don't think I'd call it anything.

ART
I see.

NARRATOR
Gwen sticks out her tongue, which Art also
remembers as a sign of intense concentration, which
she used to exhibit in a rather frightening way both on
the dance floor and when studying trigonometry, or
his trigonometry, which she used to help him with.
He never could keep his sines and cosines straight,
while she could solve differential equations in her
head. He had been very proud to be able to spell
differential.

GWEN
If I call my mood something, it will send it off in one
direction or another. And this mood is something that
needs to go where it's going and I need to wait until it
gets there. Like my train.

ART
Would you like me to wait with you?

GWEN
As it turns out. As it turns out, I would like that very
much. I never drink coffee this late. Now I'll be up all
night. Which might be just as well considering how
late my train may or may not be.

ART
Why the train? Just curious.

GWEN

I always travel by train.

ART

Why?

GWEN

Why? I don't know. I like the getting there. Instead of just the arriving.

ART

I like the train too.

GWEN

Really? Why?

ART

They travel in lines. No arcs. No parabolas through the sky. No short cuts across the earth. Here to there. I'm a here-to-there kind of guy.

GWEN

You always were.

ART

Was I? I don't think of myself that way.

GWEN

You always were. Trust me.

ART

How about you?

GWEN

Here to there? Not so much. Or. I don't know. Maybe. In a not uncomplicated way.

ART

I meant. Are you what you always were?

GWEN
What do you think?

ART
With you? I think there is no past tense.

GWEN
More likely subjunctive.

ART
If only that were true.

GWEN
You're a writer. It's your job to know these things.

ART
The more I write, the more I think my job is not to
know anything.

GWEN
Stop writing.

ART
Now there, past tense is appropriate.

GWEN
You can't stop writing.

ART
Why not?

GWEN
How will we know what happens next?

ART
Maybe nothing will.

NARRATOR
She kisses him. She was the only person he ever knew
who could smile and kiss at the same time, and he

knew it revealed something about her, something
never explained but essential to her.

GWEN

You never know.

ART

You never do.

GWEN

So you don't like past tense and you don't like
subjunctive and you don't like future tense. What will
you write?

ART

Screenplays.

GWEN

I could see that.

ART

Conditional. Story of my life. Are you okay?

NARRATOR

Gwen takes her time in answering, both to decide
what to tell, and to decide what the answer is. It is
such a simple question—and like most such questions
it does not have a simple answer.

GWEN

I'm alive.

ART

Is that an answer?

GWEN

It's the only answer I know.

NARRATOR

Art pauses, wondering if he should pursue it,
wondering if he has the right to know more,
wondering if she is right that it is the only answer.

ART

Okay, what shall we do while we wait?

GWEN

Let's talk about you.

ART

Me? That is a very short story. I hope you don't have
long to wait.

GWEN

According to the clock, I haven't been waiting at all.

ART

I mean, there's not much to tell. I live in the town I
grew up in. And I write books.

GWEN

Never married?

ART

No. I proposed once.

GWEN

Sorry. Children?

ART

Yes, actually.

GWEN

Really? You scoundrel you.

NARRATOR

Gwen is surprised. When she had thought of him over
the years, she had always imagined him married. His

wife was a schoolteacher, English probably, or maybe a professor of literature at a local college. He was a novelist, with frequent appearances on talk shows and college campuses. They had two kids, a boy and a girl, and lived in the old Jenkins farmhouse on the hill, which they named Orchard House after Louisa May Alcott, who was her favorite writer (next to him).

Though she also imagined that if he had married, one of her friends from the town would have told her, or her father would have heard and let her know. They were one of those famous couples in high school that were forever linked in the minds of classmates, regardless of reality or subsequent events, even though they had not started dating until his senior year. They were Art and Gwen. The golden couple. Or one of them. They had stayed together a long time, longer she realized than any of her marriages, through high school and sophomore year for her, though at different colleges. She lived in a dorm, but he had an apartment and she stayed with him on weekends when she could. Then junior year abroad somehow ended everything. She hadn't expected it, but she wasn't heart-broken either, probably because she didn't really believe it, that they would not be together when she returned. So many years ago. How can you know what you felt back then? Unless of course you wrote it down and put it in your novel.

ART
Yes, that's me. Scoundrel.

GWEN
Blackguard.

ART

Rascal.

GWEN

Dastard.

ART

Excuse me? Oh, dastard. I like the sound of that
actually.

GWEN

Okay, enough literary posturing. Tell me the story.

ART

I'm not sure I can tell a story without literary
posturing. I'd be thrown out of the Literary Fiction
guild. We're very self-important.

GWEN

Just this once. Between us and Merle.

ART

I was living with someone. We weren't married. And
she had a child. who was sharp and bright, and funny,
and. And wise. Wiser than I was. And I adored her. So
I unofficially adopted her.

GWEN

And her mother?

ART

Her mother and I split up after a couple of years. But.
She's still my daughter. She lives on the West Coast
now. But when she comes east, I get to see her.

GWEN

See. Was that so hard?

ART
I'll let you know after the next guild meeting.

NARRATOR
Gwen swivels and relaxes against his shoulder. She
was always touching him, he remembers. And he
never once complained, he thinks, smiling. He relaxes
into it. It feels natural. Good. She was always that way.
Natural. No barriers. Nothing between you and what
she thought and felt. What a gift to have, and to
experience, he thinks, knowing he will never, could
never, be that way, and wondering what it is like to be
that way and be with someone like him. And he
realizes then that he is picturing them together again,
and immediately raises his own barriers, which had
somehow lowered in the few minutes of
conversation. Somewhere on their walk, he thought,
maybe just where they had passed in front of the
clock, he had stopped for one moment thinking so
much.

GWEN
You're lucky.

ART
I know. You?

GWEN
Not lucky. Not in that way.

ART
I'm sorry.

GWEN
I am too sometimes. But. Not often. It's like. Do you
miss being able to leap tall buildings at a single bound?
Well, no, it sounds nice, but I never had it in my life,

so I don't miss it. I wonder sometimes what it would have been like. But even that, not often. Did you want kids?

ART
Never occurred to me, honestly. Until it happened.

GWEN
I think.

NARRATOR
She turns to him. The loss of the tiny pressure of her head against his shoulder, leaves him bereft.

GWEN
I think that is the way life should be. We shouldn't say life is meaningless without—whatever. Life is never meaningless, because it was never meant to be meaningful. That's us, that's our culture, our parents, our teachers telling us. But it's not true. We have no idea what life is supposed to be, because it's not supposed to be anything. Our species is a few hundred thousand years old, our language is far younger than that. How can we possibly think we have the words to explain life? Maybe some species billions of years from now. But I doubt it.

ART
See. Pensive.

GWEN
No. Just a lot of time to read on the train. Okay. Maybe. So. No marriages. One child. How many books have you written?

ART
26.

GWEN
Don't get out much, do you?

ART
Visits from old friends are few and far between.

(She punches him on the arm)

GWEN
That's for using the O word.

NARRATOR
She reaches into her bag and pulls out his book again.
She turns to the back of the book.

GWEN
I thought I had read them all, but I haven't read
anywhere near 26. It lists six here.

ART
Only six of them are published.

GWEN
Six? Why? You're so good.

ART
Thank you. It's the way of the publishing world. Six
published is good. Six is a lot.

GWEN
Wow. So you have seventeen books sitting in a
drawer.

ART
Actually, they're in the Cloud, but yes, metaphorically
speaking.

GWEN
Are they good?

ART
They are—well-written.

GWEN
That sounds like a no.

ART
They aspire to sound like good books.

GWEN
I'd like to read them.

ART
I don't think...

GWEN
What?

ART
I don't think I want you to remember me as the
person who wrote them.

GWEN
Why is that important?

ART
I don't know. It wasn't an hour ago. An hour ago, I
would have been happy for anyone to ask to read
them. Though I still would have probably said no. I
haven't read most of them in years. I can't vouch for
them, I guess I am saying.

GWEN
I can see that. I get it. Still. 26 books in mphmfh years.
That's an accomplishment.

ART
Of a sort, I suppose.

GWEN

It's impressive to me. I struggle with Christmas cards.

ART

So do I.

GWEN

Really? So. One thing we have in common.

ART

Meant for each other.

GWEN

Absolutely. We were meant to not write Christmas cards together until the end of time.

ART

It's something.

GWEN

Not exactly Heathcliff and Cathy.

NARRATOR

Art's eyebrows climb half an inch on his face. A new gesture, she thinks. And she realizes she is cataloging them, storing them in an archive in case this is the last time they meet. She wonders why she cares so much. She has no expectations, no hopes, not even much curiosity where he is concerned, none that she is aware of anyway. But she seldom dives into the depths of herself seeking answers, since she had learned over the years that even if the answers existed they could not be found amid the foggy morass that constitutes her leftover life. She has never been a planner, as he was. What is his plan for tonight? she wonders. She knows he has one. But for some reason, she does not dare to ask. Very unlike her, who dares most anything as a matter of course, since she has at this point in her life nothing to lose that she would mourn. Except, perhaps, now she does, she thinks. A misunderstanding, a lost love, and a life misled because of it. That at least would be something to mourn, something to think about on the long train trip back to. Back to where? Trains never take you back. They only take you forward.

His eyebrows lowered. Heathcliff and Cathy was not a comparison he would have thought of, nor aspired to. Though he preferred to view the universe through literary archetypes. Who were they? he wondered. Not Romeo and Juliet certainly. Beatrice and Benedict possibly. Antony and Cleopatra? No. He thought of his own books. He had attempted to write them before, several times. None really captured who they were now. He brightened. A new book, he thinks. Possibly.

ART
It's the 21ˢᵗ century equivalent.

GWEN
Hmm. This does seem to be an unromantic century so far.

ART
There's still time.

GWEN
For the century, true.

ART
And for us.

GWEN
You think so?

ART

I'm not ready to rule it out.

GWEN

By us, do you mean you and me or do you mean us?

ART

I mean you and me.

ART

But I'm not ruling out us either. We are having delicious coffee alone in a train station. That seems potentially romantic.

GWEN

Only to a romantic. Makes me wonder about those unpublished books.

ART

Ask.

GWEN

Did they have happy endings?

ART

I suppose you could say that. In a Dante-ish sort of way.

NARRATOR

Gwen picks up his book, turns the book around and holds it up next to his head, comparing the picture on the back cover to his face now. She likes the real face better. The warmly perplexed eyes and the lips prepared to curve at any moment. Then she closes the book decisively, the better to argue her point.

GWEN

Who is your favorite writer?

ART
Other than me?

GWEN
Other than you.

ART
Actually, we don't have to exclude me. There are
many books I'd rather read than mine.

GWEN
It's not the same thing, is it?

ART
What do you mean?

GWEN
Books you'd rather read.

NARRATOR
She makes air quotes (and he notices her hands for
the first time—shapely, no wrinkles or blemishes,
with delicate whitish pink nails—and this subsumes
him in memory of her touch, all of them, overlaid,
merged into the memory of a single touch, and for a
brief moment he is overwhelmed by ancient desire
and barely stops himself from reaching for her, then
the feeling evaporates, hurricane become mist)

GWEN
Is different from favorite writer.

NARRATOR
Again with the air quotes and the process begins and
ends again, leaving him breathless.

GWEN
Art?

                    Art
Gwen?

                    Narrator
Art and Gwen, they both think, for the first time. Art
and Gwen. There is a power in the mythos of those
names. Their names conjoined are a charm. Her hand
encircles his wrist, not quite taking his pulse, which is
racing.

                    Gwen
Are you okay? Not having a heart attack, are you?

                    Art
My heart is fine.

                    Gwen
Good. Because I don't know CPR. I do know the
Heimlich Maneuver.

                    Art
Noted.

                    Gwen
No. They are not the same.

                    Art
The Heimlich Maneuver is not the same as CPR?

                    Gwen
No, a book you want to read most is not the same as
favorite writer. Because a book you would rather read
is affected by other factors, like how tired you are or
what mood you're in.

                    Gwen
Favorite writer is the writer whose books mean the
most to you.

ART

Oh. Well. Then I am my favorite writer, but I'd rather read anyone else's books instead of mine.

GWEN

Why?

ART

I don't know about other writers, but by the time I finish one of mine I am sick of it. The only page of it I want to open is the one I sign my name to at a bookstore. Or train station.

GWEN

Your books, the published ones anyway, are warm and entertaining and thoughtful. I like them very much.

ART

Thank you for the blurb. I'll add it to my marketing material. You are my target demographic.

GWEN

You mean women of a certain age?

ART

No. I mean you. I always write for you. Though I'm not sure if it's the you I remember or the you I imagine.

NARRATOR

He watches her face carefully, tracking the evolution, in the eyes, which unfocus and focus twice, in the line in the jaw, which softens and firms in conjunction, and the arc of the lips. Especially the arc of the lips. The arc of her lips. He wanted so much at that instant to test it out, to kiss her again, as her lips curved, and maybe finally solve that mystery, her mystery, which had remained unsolved for so many years. But it wasn't that kind of meeting. Was it? Did he even want it to be? Now, yes, But a moment from now?

> GWEN

Really. Well. Good job.

> ART

Thank you.

> NARRATOR

He knows he has lost a chance. He would not have the courage now. They have achieved something, and he fears he would disturb it, cancel it, whatever it is.

> GWEN

No one's ever written anything for me before. Much less 26 books. Wait, that's not true. I got a postcard once. But it was from my mother.

> ART

What did it say?

> GWEN

It didn't say anything. I suppose it was meant to be sort of proof of life.

> ART

I think that's what my books are. Proof of life.

> GWEN

It's better than a postcard.

> ART

In scale.

> GWEN

Now you're just being modest.

ART
They teach that at Author School too.

GWEN
Hey Merle. Who's your favorite author?

MERLE
My favorite or the one I like to read most?

GWEN
Who's your favorite?

MERLE
Tolstoy.

GWEN
Really?

MERLE
In Russian. You have to read Tolstoy in Russian.

GWEN
You speak Russian?

MERLE
Ya uznal ot babushki. Ona by ne vyuchila angliyskiy.

GWEN
Ya ne vinyu yeye.

MERLE
You speak Russian.

GWEN
Da.

ART
Hey Merle. Why Tolstoy?

MERLE
I only read one book a year, so it needs to last.

ART
There's Proust.

MERLE
I don't drink tea.

ART
Joyce.

MERLE
Juvenile sense of humor.

ART
And you find Tolstoy funny?

MERLE
In Russian, he's hilarious.

ART
So Tolstoy. Fine choice. War and Peace?

MERLE
That's good. But I prefer Anna Karenina.

GWEN
Me too. Has trains in it.

ART
True. Not a happy ending though.

GWEN
You'll just have to write your version.

NARRATOR
Art once more glances at the clock, then at her, then back at the clock, then at his phone, then back at the clock.

ART
Why don't they fix that clock? Hey Merle?

MERLE

Yeah?

ART

Why don't they fix that clock?

MERLE

Cause everybody has a phone now. Nobody even
looks at it nowadays.

ART

Hey Merle?

MERLE

Yeah?

ART

Have you got a ladder?

GWEN

Art?

ART

Gwen?

NARRATOR

She smiles. This intensity she knows. He had this all
through the time they dated. At this point, if an
earthquake destroyed the station around him, he
would search through the rubble for the clock and fix
it. Though he would scoop her up first and get her to
safety. She had met many men in her life. None had
that ability (or sometimes disability) to focus on
something, or someone, so intensely everything else
dropped away. Possibly why he could write so many
books, that focus. She had never had a problem
getting men's attention, though often getting men's
attention was a problem in itself. But she remembered

his face when he looked at her that way; as though he saw her completely, and through her completely. And in doing so, he also opened all of himself to you. When you were the object of that all-encompassing attention, it was unnerving, and exciting. But now the object of that attention was the clock on the wall, and she is afraid.

GWEN
Don't hurt yourself.

ART
I'm just going to reset it. Maybe that will get it started. Where's the ladder, Merle?

MERLE
In the closet. But I'm not sure it's tall enough.

ART
We'll see.

MERLE
I don't think the station insurance covers this. Actually, I don't think there is any station insurance.

GWEN
You don't need to do this. It won't make a difference. The train will come when it comes.

ART
It makes a difference. Not to the train, no. But it makes a difference.

GWEN
I guess it does. Go for it!

NARRATOR

Art places the ladder beneath the clock and starts to
climb. Gwen rushes over to steady the ladder. He
climbs the ladder. Merle sidles up to the ladder and
grabs one side, while she grabs the other. Arts reaches
up, slips his hand behind the clock and finds the knob.

ART

What time is it now?

GWEN

Hold on.

GWEN

Three fourteen and a little.

NARRATOR

He twists the knob clockwise, but the hands go
backward. He twists it counterclockwise, and the
hands spin forward, finally reaching three fourteen.
Art climbs carefully down the ladder and reaches the
floor. They all stare up at the clock, hoping it will
move. Nothing happens. Then Merle walks to the wall
and flips a switch. The second hand starts to turn.

MERLE

They turned it off in 2011. The clock always ran fast
anyway.

ART

They usually do.

NARRATOR

She smiles, but the smile is interrupted as the train
whistle sounds. She rushes back to the bench, and
begins collecting her things. He follows.

GWEN

That's my train. I hope.

ART

Do you?

GWEN

Less than I did before.

ART

I'm glad I got to see you again.

GWEN

You are still an interesting man. Wait.

ART

What?

GWEN

The world is a sphere.

ART

So?

GWEN

The surface of a sphere is an arc.

ART

And?

GWEN

So trains travel in arcs.

ART

Huh. I think I'll buy a ticket.

GWEN

Why?

ART

Hey Merle?

MERLE
Yes?

ART
Do you have baseball caps for sale?

MERLE
Yeah, sure. Yankees. Red Sox. Mets. That's from 1986.

ART
86 Mets? That's perfect. How much?

MERLE
Take it. You're doing me a Favor.

NARRATOR
Art offers it to Gwen. She hesitates, then spins her hair into a ponytail and puts on the cap.

ART
Perfect. And there's one more reason.

GWEN
Which is?

ART
I need to check out this arc thing. Could be a whole new world.

GWEN
But you don't know where I'm going.

ART
Here to there. Where else is there?

GWEN
Let's find out. Thank you, Merle. See you next trip.

NARRATOR
Gwen and Art exit together under the clock and
through the doors to the station platform just as the
train is pulling in. Merle sits back on his stool, takes
up the crossword again.

MERLE
Unusual. Rare. Extraordinary. U-N-W-O-N-T-E-D.

NARRATOR
Merle looks at the double doors to the track, then up
at the clock, where the second hand is now born
ceaselessly into the future.

MERLE
Must have been the mints.

Lights fade.

The End

No Surprise

A Play in One Act

"I meant to write about death, only life came breaking in as usual."

Virginia Woolf
Diary, February 17, 1922

Cast of Characters

A Clerk   Any age

A Person   Any age

Scene

Unknown.

Time

Eternity.

Act I Scene 1

Setting: A bare stage, except for a desk
downstage center. Up left is a doorway.
A bright light shines through it.

At Rise: A clerk is sitting at the desk, waiting,
hands folded.

*A Person enters, wanders around a bit, then
approaches the desk.*

CLERK
Welcome to Death.

PERSON
Where?

CLERK
Death.

Person nods.

PERSON
Where?

CLERK
Death. This is Death.

PERSON
So I'm dead?

CLERK
You people. Everything is all about you.

PERSON
Excuse me?

CLERK
That is one possibility.

PERSON
Excuse me?

CLERK
If you insist.

PERSON
Pardon?

CLERK
Well, that's a little more challenging.

PERSON
I don't think I understand.

CLERK
If you think, you don't understand.

PERSON
Excuse me?

CLERK
You're persistent. I'll give you that.

PERSON
Pardon?

CLERK
Anything is possible.

PERSON
So.

CLERK
Yep.

PERSON

And back when.

CLERK

Oh yeah.

PERSON

And then I.

CLERK

I would say so.

PERSON

So now.

CLERK

Almost there.

PERSON

This is.

CLERK

You can do it.

PERSON

Death.

CLERK

Hallelujah!

PERSON

Death?

CLERK

I knew you had it in you.

PERSON

Death?

CLERK

When you first entered, I thought to myself that is a person who has it in them.

                    PERSON
Death?

                    CLERK
Naturally.

                    PERSON
Death.

                    CLERK
Think nothing of it. Or anything else for that matter.

                    PERSON
I don't understand.

                    CLERK
That's because you have it in you.

                    PERSON
What is it?

                    CLERK
Obviously.

                    PERSON
So. This is death.

                    CLERK
This is death.

                    PERSON
And you are?

                    CLERK
Obviously.

                    PERSON
You don't have to be sarcastic.

                    CLERK
Oh. There is no sarcasm in Death.

PERSON

I see.

CLERK

That was sarcastic.

PERSON

I see.

CLERK

Just thought I'd mention that.

PERSON

I see.

CLERK

But sarcasm is not encouraged.

PERSON

Death isn't funny.

CLERK

Oh no. Comedy is encouraged. Death is very funny.

PERSON

So you say.

CLERK

So what can I do for you?

PERSON

I don't know. I just got here.

The clerk laughs. For a long time.

CLERK

That's a good one. I have to remember that one. "I just got here".

PERSON

What can you do for me?

CLERK
What can't I do?

PERSON
I don't know. There seem to be a lot of rules.

CLERK
I wouldn't call them rules. More like improbabilities.

PERSON
I see. So what is probable?

CLERK
Likely.

PERSON
So what is likely?

CLERK
Probably.

PERSON
I don't think we're getting anywhere here.

CLERK
That anywhere is here is improbable.

PERSON
I'm not sure we're communicating.

CLERK
Who can say?

PERSON
So. Let me recap. I'm dead.

CLERK
Well done. Now that's what I call communication.

PERSON
I'm dead.

CLERK
Clear. Succinct. Almost true.

PERSON
Almost true?

CLERK
Very close. I would say really really in the vicinity.
Except for the part that's wrong.

PERSON
Which part is that?

CLERK
The 'm.

PERSON
The 'm?

CLERK
Mmm.

PERSON
Mmm?

CLERK
Mmm.

PERSON
Hmmm

CLERK
No. Mmm.

PERSON
I think I've lost the thread.

CLERK
Then you don't need the needle.

PERSON
Needle?

CLERK
Or the camel. That's a myth.

PERSON
Are you saying I'm not dead?

CLERK
I was saying that. I'm not anymore.

PERSON
I'm not dead.

CLERK
I could say it again if it's helpful.

PERSON
Would you please?

CLERK
We are all about customer service. You. Are. Not.
Dead.

PERSON
I'm not dead.

CLERK
Nope.

PERSON
But this is death?

CLERK
Yep.

PERSON
Death is.

CLERK
Obviously.

PERSON
Death is?

CLERK

You can do it!

PERSON

Death is a place?

CLERK

Can I get a ruling on that one?

The Clerk looks offstage and waits.

CLERK

Okay, we're going to give you that one. Ontologically it's a little shaky, but close enough.

PERSON

Death is a place.

CLERK

Think of it as "death is where you're at?" It helps if you lived during the 60s.

PERSON

I see.

CLERK

I'm glad.

PERSON

You said 'm.

CLERK

Oh let's not start that again.

PERSON

Finally we agree on something.

CLERK

And we agree on something final.

PERSON

So this is death.

CLERK
Yes.

PERSON
It's not what I expected.

CLERK
I expect not.

PERSON
I thought, maybe, angels. Choirs. Heavenly hosts.

CLERK
They're on break.

PERSON
Really?

CLERK
See, I told you sarcasm doesn't work here.

PERSON
I see what you mean.

CLERK
You can't see what I mean. I don't mean what can be seen.

PERSON
Well. It was a good life I guess.

CLERK
Really?

PERSON
On balance. Mostly. A lot.

CLERK
So you were a good person?

PERSON
On balance. Mostly. A lot.

CLERK
Good. I assume that's good.

PERSON
Don't you know? Isn't there some book somewhere
that tells you, adds up the plusses and minuses and
calculates the Goodness of my life?

CLERK
We try not to make those kinds of judgements.

PERSON
Oh.

CLERK
We leave that up to you.

PERSON
Oh. Oh?

CLERK
So?

PERSON
You're asking me if I was a good person?

CLERK
That was your criteria.

PERSON
What happens if I wasn't? Do I go to Hell?

CLERK
That's up to you.

PERSON
It's up to me?

The clerk shrugs.

CLERK

Think of me as a travel agent. I don't decide where you go, I just help you get there.

PERSON

So I will go somewhere?

CLERK

Again that's up to you.

PERSON

So how long do I have to stay here?

CLERK

We don't really like to deal in timeframes.

PERSON

Why?

CLERK

Because there aren't any.

PERSON

Why not?

CLERK

Because there isn't any time here.

PERSON

I'm here forever?

CLERK

You're here always. But not forever.

PERSON

Let's assume I understand that. So you're saying I have a choice?

CLERK

Do you want one?

PERSON
Yes.

CLERK
Are you sure?

PERSON
Yes.

CLERK
How did your last choice work out?

PERSON
Which choice?

CLERK
Life. How did that work out?

PERSON
I chose life?

CLERK
You were alive, correct?

PERSON
I was.

CLERK
Then you chose it.

PERSON
Why do you want to know?

CLERK
I'm curious.

PERSON
I'm just an average person.

CLERK
Then I'm really curious. I've never met one before.

PERSON
What? You must have met thousands.

CLERK
Uncounted multitudes. But never anyone average.
Being average is incredibly rare.

PERSON
How long have you been here?

CLERK
I've been here since Always.

PERSON
That's confusing.

CLERK
Only if you think about it.

PERSON
Good point.

CLERK
I understand that you are experiencing this
sequentially. But don't worry. You'll get over that.

PERSON
In time?

CLERK
Oh no.

*Pause. Person is very confused. Clerk just smiles.
Then get serious.*

CLERK
So. How was life?

PERSON
You must know. You must have been alive sometime.

CLERK
No. Never made it to life.

PERSON
You were never alive?

CLERK
I don't think so.

PERSON
Then how did you get here?

CLERK
I applied online.

PERSON
No I mean. If you weren't born, why do you exist?

CLERK
One has nothing to do with the other.

PERSON
Really?

CLERK
As far as I know.

PERSON
Don't you know?

CLERK
You hear stories.

PERSON
Then you're not God?

CLERK
God I hope not. I would be really underpaid.

PERSON
Is there a God?

CLERK
You hear stories.

PERSON
So you have never met God?

CLERK
Not that I know of. I'm not sure I'd recognize it if I did.

PERSON
God is an it?

CLERK
In English. English doesn't have Eternal Pronouns. Yet.

PERSON
Are we speaking English?

CLERK
No, we're speaking American. I can speak English if you would like.

PERSON
No, that's okay.

CLERK
It would just muddy up the communication. We're already having a hard enough time.

PERSON
American is fine.

CLERK
So tell me about life?

PERSON
So. Life. What can I say? Its more interesting than death.

CLERK

Tell me about it.

PERSON

Things happen one after another.

CLERK

Wow. Imagine that. What else?

PERSON

And once something happens, we don't know the next thing that's going to happen. Sometimes we think we know. But we can never be sure.

CLERK

That thinking thing seems like a real problem.

PERSON

It can be.

CLERK

Why do you do it?

PERSON

Once you start it's hard to stop.

CLERK

Ah.

PERSON

What else? What else? Well, we start out small and get bigger.

CLERK

As your brains expand from all the thinking.

PERSON

Not really. Actually we start losing brains cells as we age.

CLERK

Oh. Sorry.

PERSON

So. What else can I tell you? It's hard to talk about life with someone who hasn't lived.

CLERK

I can see that. Well, tell me this. Were you happy?

PERSON

Happy? Happy. Hmmm. Now that I think of it—

CLERK

Careful. Don't want your head to explode.

PERSON

Not likely. I guess. All in all. I wasn't happy. So much.

CLERK

I see.

PERSON

I mean. I did things. I loved people. I did things to people I loved.

CLERK

Love. I've heard of that. What is love?

PERSON

It's where you think of someone more than you think yourself.

CLERK

So love comes from thinking.

PERSON

No, come to think of it.

CLERK

So love comes from not thinking.

PERSON
No. You know. It's like. How to describe it. You know. You know. Like in the books.

CLERK
There are no books here.

PERSON
No books?

CLERK
No stories at all.

PERSON
No stories at all?

CLERK
None. Stories are a sequential effect. You need that one thing after another thing in a story.

PERSON
I would miss stories I think.

CLERK
Did they make you happy?

PERSON
No. But they made me forget I was unhappy.

CLERK
I'm sorry you weren't happy. Maybe next time.

PERSON
Next time. So there is a next time?

CLERK
Could be.

PERSON
So death isn't the end. It just keeps going. Forever. It never stops.

CLERK
As it will be in the beginning, was now, and ever used to be. Unless.

PERSON
Unless?

CLERK
You could have my job.

PERSON
Your job?

CLERK
I think you'd be good at it.

PERSON
Your job?

CLERK
You're a pleasant sort of person.

PERSON
Thank you.

CLERK
You're not very good at explaining things. But that is not really one of the criteria for the job.

PERSON
So I noticed.

CLERK
It's a good job really. You meet lots of interesting beings. It's a comfy chair. It swivels. Which is fun when things slow down. They'll say they'll work on the wifi.

PERSON
I don't think it's for me.

CLERK
There you go thinking again.

PERSON
Sorry.

CLERK
Where has that ever gotten you?

PERSON
Death?

CLERK
Exactly.

PERSON
I see what...I see.

CLERK
Stories. You like stories. We get some very good storytellers here. Aeschylus. Shakespeare. Rod Serling.

PERSON
Really?

CLERK
Yeah, he would have been great at this job. Had just the right voice.

PERSON
Oh yeah.

CLERK
I mean. Think about the life you just lived. Don't you want something new?

PERSON
Maybe. If it is such a good job, why would you give it up?

                    CLERK
Fair question.

                    PERSON
I think so.

                    CLERK
Honestly, I'm tired of never being surprised.

                    PERSON
Really?

                    CLERK
Yeah. I mean it's nice that I never forget to buy
orange juice. But there is never anything new.
Nothing changes. Everything always is.

                    PERSON
Not all surprises are pleasant, you know. For instance,
death was a bit of a shock.

                    CLERK
I suppose. But. It is something I have never
experienced. I only know everything. I mean, like
stories. To not know how something ends. I can
hardly imagine that.

                    PERSON
But you might not be happy. I wasn't.

                    CLERK
True. And I am happy here. Nothing happens.

                    PERSON
If I took the job, could I get out of it and go
somewhere else?

                    CLERK
Sure. You just need someone to take your place.

PERSON
Ah. So that's it. You need me to say yes.

CLERK
Yes.

PERSON
I could stand a little happiness.

CLERK
More than a little. An eternity of happiness.

PERSON
Okay it's a deal.

They shake hands.

PERSON
Hey wait. you knew I would say yes didn't you?

CLERK
I did. Here. Take a seat.

*Person sits in the chair, undergoes the transition
to eternal knowledge.*

PERSON
So. Where would you like to go?

CLERK
I don't know. I don't know! How about that? I don't
know something?

PERSON
Can I make a suggestion?

CLERK
Sure. That's your job now.

PERSON
Give life a try. If you pay attention, everything will surprise you.

CLERK
You know. It wouldn't surprise me.

PERSON
Okay then. See you next death.

Clerk waves and exits.

PERSON
Next!

Clerk enters, wanders around a bit, then approaches the desk.

PERSON
Welcome to Death.

Blackout

The End

About the Playwright

Stephen Evans is a playwright and the author of *The Island of Always, Whose Beauty is Past Change,* and *Funny Thing Is: A Guide to Understanding Comedy.*

Find him online at:

https://www.istephenevans.com/

STEPHEN EVANS

Books by Stephen Evans

Plays:

The Visitation Quartet:
    The Ghost Writer
    Monuments
    Tourists
    Spooky Action at a Distance
    At the Still Point

Experience	*Three plays about Ralph Waldo Emerson*
Generations	*(with Morey Norkin and Michael Gilles)*
As You Like It	*(by William Shakespeare, adapted by Stephen Evans)*
The Glass Door	*(An adaptation of Hedda Gabler by Henrik Ibsen)*

Non-Fiction:

Funny Thing Is: *A Guide to Understanding Comedy*
Anthropomorphosis
Small Gifts
Liebestraum
The Laughing String: Thoughts on Writing

STEPHEN EVANS

STEPHEN EVANS

S<small>TEPHEN</small> E<small>VANS</small>